Classic Cars

By James Buckley Jr.

The **Child's World**
www.childsworld.com

Published in the United States of America by The Child's World®
1980 Lookout Drive • Mankato, MN 56003-1705
800-599-READ • www.childsworld.com

Many thanks to young car fan Conor Buckley for his inspiration
and assistance in choosing these classics!

ACKNOWLEDGMENTS

The Child's World®: Mary Berendes, Publishing Director

Produced by Shoreline Publishing Group LLC
President / Editorial Director: James Buckley, Jr.
Designer: Tom Carling, carlingdesign.com
Cover Art: Slimfilms
Assistant Editor: Jim Gigliotti

Photo Credits:
Cover: iStock, Photos.com
Interior: All photos from Kimball Stock except the
following: Dreamstime.com/Bill Philpot 7. Photos.com: 5;
Shoreline Publishing Group 9, 10, 26, 28 bottom.

LIBRARY OF CONGRESS CATALOG-IN-PUBLICATION DATA

Buckley, James, 1963–
    Classic cars / by James Buckley Jr.
        p. cm.—(Reading rocks!)
    Includes index.
    ISBN 978-1-60253-095-9 (library bound : alk. paper)
    1. Antique and classic cars—Juvenile literature. I. Title. II.
Series.

TL147.B799 2008
629.222--dc22

2008006052

CONTENTS

1

HERE COME THE Classics

Cars were invented in the late 1800s. The first cars were a bit boring. They were simple, black, and boxy, and had very few features. In a few years, European carmakers began combining gold and art on rolling masterpieces. Only rich people could afford such cars, however. "Regular" drivers didn't have many shapes or colors to choose from.

Two things helped change that: World War II (1939–1945) and the U.S. highway system. In the years following the war, many Americans found

that they could afford something a little nicer than a Model T. Car designers were inspired by super-fast planes from the war, too.

The highway system was growing quickly. Americans wanted a fun way to use the new highways. The age of "classic cars" was beginning. Strap on your seatbelt and let's check them out!

Up until the 1940s, most cars were boxes. They were boring. Then, suddenly—**chrome!** Cars from several makers in the late 1940s and early 1950s added splashes of the shiny silver metal.

The Buick Skylark is a good example. This beautiful, curving

The Buick Skylark was one of the first cars to use a lot of shiny chrome.

two-door car had chrome around the windows, on the **grill**, and in a stripe along the sides. Even the wheels had chrome **spokes**!

The 1948 Cadillac Coupe de Ville added another new part to American cars: tail fins. The 1948 **model** was the first to have these small, raised metal tabs at the top edges of the car's rear section. Like everything else in America at the time, tail fins just kept getting bigger and bigger. By 1959, the Cadillac El Dorado convertible had tail fins that were almost one foot (30 cm) tall. Each fin had its own taillight.

The tail fins on this 1958 Cadillac were so big, each one had two taillights!

Here's a peek at the Chevy's V-8 engine. It made the car both powerful and easy to drive.

In an engine, the cylinders hold pistons, which are metal rods that move up and down very quickly. The rods turn a longer rod which turns the wheels. In a V-8, the eight cylinders are set up in a V shape, with four on each side.

For three years in the mid-1950s, Chevrolet combined all that was good about American cars at the time. The car Chevy came up with remains one of the most famous cars ever made—the Bel Air.

The Bel Air boasted a powerful **V-8 engine**, with eight **cylinders**. These cars were priced so that a regular family could afford one, too. Big, fancy, smooth-driving cars were no longer out of reach for the average buyer.

Of course, the Bel Air also looked totally cool! Nice tail fins, lots of chrome, plenty of room inside and . . . it came in a dozen great colors! There was even a station-wagon version known as the Nomad. Few cars say "America" as clearly as the classic Chevy Bel Air.

"Chevy" is short for Chevrolet.

Collectors show off their classic Bel Airs at car shows.

Put the top down in your T-Bird and feel the wind in your hair!

Carmakers weren't just building **sedans** in the 1950s. Americans were being treated to new sports cars, too. Sports cars were smaller, faster, and had sleeker designs. Many Americans loved the family freedom of the Bel Air sedan, but some people wanted a bit more style. For them, Ford made the Thunderbird sports car.

The Ford Thunderbird took American car style into the future. Known as the "T-Bird," the two-seat version remains one of the most famous American cars ever made. The models made from 1955 to 1957 are some of the most popular among car collectors. The T-Bird's combination of a long hood and a short back made it perfect.

Woody Wagon

The classic family station wagon of this time was the "Woody Wagon" from Mercury and Ford. With room for eight, the Woody had wooden panels on its side, as well as wood trim inside. Many surf-loving teens "loaded up the Woody" to head to the beach.

2

MAKE WAY FOR Muscle Cars

Big fins, lots of chrome, and a classic style. That was all fine for some people, but lots of car lovers also wanted power—they wanted speed! American carmakers granted this wish in the early 1960s.

The "muscle car" was created for people who wanted clean **lines**, all the extra features of a passenger car, and speed. Muscle cars put big, powerful V-8 engines in great-looking cars—at a price many people could afford.

The first muscle car was the Chevrolet Impala 409 SS. Known today simply as the 409, it was so popular that the Beach Boys wrote a song about it! Its 409 **cubic-inch** engine was inspired by drag racers. For the first time, speed lovers could enjoy a comfortable car!

The 409 was not that fancy, but it was faster than just about any other car.

The sounds of the Impala's engine were soon joined on America's roads by another classic. In 1964, Pontiac made the GTO. It was the perfect mix of power and cool—plus you could fit four people inside!

Foreign sports cars were considered to be too small and expensive. Bigger sedans didn't

Riding this powerful kind of "Goat" was a pretty cool way to get around in the 1960s!

excite people who wanted a cool, fast car, either. To give these drivers what they wanted, Pontiac took its Tempest passenger-car model and added a huge engine and other features.

The GTO included a powerful 389 cubic-inch V-8 engine, and it could rocket from 0 to 60 mph (97 kph) in 7.5 seconds.

The GTO, also known as "The Goat," was a huge hit among muscle-car fans from the start. Many collectors are proud to own them today—but they might pay more than $100,000 for good ones! Collectors still think the original GTOs are the best.

Pontiac took the name GTO from a type of Ferrari made in Italy. The initials stand for *Gran Turismo Omologato,* which means "grand touring model."

Muscle cars were a big hit with car fans. But what about the average person? Ford came up with an answer in 1964, and the result is still seen on roads today.

The Mustang created a class of cars known as "pony cars." Why pony? A mustang is a type of horse!

Ford created the Mustang as an affordable, sporty car. It was not as powerful as the GTO, but it was a car that a young couple or even a small family could buy. Its styling was that of a sports car **merged** with a muscle car. It had a long hood with a shorter rear section—a new look that quickly caught on.

In the first two and a half years of production, the Mustang sold more than 1.2 million cars. It quickly became an American favorite.

Many other cars, such as the Plymouth Barracuda, tried to match the Mustang, but could never touch its popularity.

Ford still makes Mustangs, but today's models look quite a bit different. Many collectors still enjoy driving and owning the original "pony car."

This classic 1966 Mustang shows off the two-colored look. The car also came in solid colors.

This Camaro Z28 was used in ceremonies at the 1969 Indianapolis 500 auto race.

In 1968, Chevy made the Camaro Z28. The car was based on Chevys from the Trans Am sports car championships. The Z28 was the **street-legal** version of a race car. Muscle-car fans were thrilled!

The Camaros looked awesome and went fast, topping out at nearly 125 mph (201 kph). Owners could also watch special models win dozens of top races.

In 1970, Dodge's Charger featured a huge 440 cubic-inch engine. It hit 60 mph (97 kph) from a standing start in 5.6 seconds! The two-door model was a big hit, selling more than 80,000 cars in 1970.

Muscle cars faded out in the mid-1970s. Drivers wanted smaller cars that didn't guzzle so much gas. New models of the Charger are back on the streets, however.

One version of the Charger included a large wing at the back.

3

STEP INTO

Sports Cars

Not all the great cars of the 1950s and 1960s were being made in the United States. European carmakers were creating cars that remain some of the most beautiful and classic sports cars of all time.

The Italian carmaker Ferrari made only 36 copies of its 1962 250 GTO model. These rare GTOs remain such amazing cars, a collector might pay more than $10 million for one! You don't have to be a car lover to appreciate its beauty, though. Plus, the 250 was

If you want to drive a Ferrari 250, bring a lot of money. These classics are among the world's most valuable cars.

one of the most successful racing sports cars of all time.

In Germany, the Porsche 365A Speedster helped **define** the two-seat sports car. Small, fast, and beautiful, the 365A was the first of many amazing Porsches.

This 365A was the first of many great sports cars made by Porsche.

Small, cute, and easy to drive—the Giulietta was a big hit in Italy.

Italy and Germany were home to other top carmakers, too. The Italian Alfa Romeo company put out a pair of sports cars that remain classics. The Giulietta came out in 1955. This tiny car was so small, it could nearly fit inside a Bel Air! But it was quick and easy to handle. The Duetto Spider followed in 1966. The Spider was small, sporty, and quick, too.

Germany's BMW company made only 253 copies of its 507 model

from 1956 to 1959. The 507 remains much-loved by experts as one of the first great sports cars.

Lamborghini dueled with Ferrari to see who made the hottest Italian cars. The 1967 Lamborghini Miura set new standards for beauty in sports cars. Its awesome V-12 engine topped out at nearly 175 mph (280 kph)! Beauty and speed—car lovers' two favorite things!

The Ferrari Miura featured air scoops on its sides to help it speed down the road.

Great Britain got into the act during these car-loving days, too. Companies like MG, Triumph, Austin-Healy, Jaguar, and Aston Martin all put out small, speedy **roadsters**. The cars all combined quick handling with smaller engines and beautiful designs.

British sports cars were very popular in the 1960s, with this MG being among the favorites.

Among the most popular was MG's "B" model, which had only four cylinders but a classic "look."

The British-made Aston Martin DB5 became famous thanks to one driver: James Bond. The famous movie spy drove a DB5 in 1964's *Goldfinger*. Fans rushed to "be like Bond," although the real models that were sold in stores didn't come with Bond's secret weapons!

The Jaguar XK120 had one of the most famous body shapes in the sports-car world. No other car sported its long, smooth lines. Jaguars continue to be among the world's most elegant cars.

After seeing movie spy James Bond drive this Aston Martin DB5, thousands of drivers wanted to be a spy, too!

The Corvette was supposed to compete with the T-Bird, but it soon surpassed it.

The United States was not missing from these sports-car years, however. For example, Chevrolet's two-seat Corvette borrowed the best parts of the European sports-car styles. Then Chevy put in a V-6, and later, a big V-8 engine. The 'Vette, as it was known, caught on and became the first really popular American sports car. It remains popular with collectors.

Chevy put out new Corvette models throughout the 1960s. Each model added another page to the legend. The key feature in Corvettes was fuel injection. Engines with this feature can generate more power, since gasoline is "sprayed" into the engine at a higher rate. This feature made Corvettes extra special.

The Stingray

Other than the original 1953s, the most famous Corvette was the Stingray. This long-body model first came out in 1963. An even longer version, the Mako Shark, came out in 1970. Why the big hood? Big engine! The 454 cubic-inch model was the largest ever put in a Chevy!

The Viper turns heads whether it's roaring by or just standing still.

Today's car lovers have many amazing machines to choose from. These wheels don't have the history of the other cars in this book, but they still turn heads.

The Dodge Viper is perhaps America's hottest sports car. Introduced in 2003, the Viper just looks fast—plus it tops out at 190 mph (306 kph). Named for the famed car designer Carroll Shelby, the Ford Shelby GT500 is a modern

Racing fans have snapped up these GT500s, hoping to get a little of the Shelby name.

muscle car. Its 505 cubic-inch engine roars, and its powerful body makes today's "regular" cars look like toys.

Finally, the Bugatti Veyron leads the world in "mosts": speed (about 260 mph/418 kph), cost ($2.1 million for the rarest model), style (just look at it!), and cylinders (16).

Only about 500 Veyrons will be made. If you want one, you might have to wait two years!

Whether you like old or new cars, keep your eyes peeled the next time you're on the road. You never know what might just make you say, "Wow! Did you see that?"

GLOSSARY

chrome a very shiny silver metal

cubic-inch a unit of measurement that measures one inch tall, one inch wide, and one inch deep

cylinders the hollow areas of an engine in which the pistons move up and down (which turn the axle, which turns the wheels)

define to tell what something is or means

foreign from another country

grill a screen at the front of a car through which air flows over an engine

lines when speaking about cars, this means the shape along the sides and top of a car

merged put together

model when speaking of cars, this means all cars with the same name

roadsters smaller, two-seat sports cars with four-cylinder engines

sedans large passenger cars that can seat at least four people

spokes metal rods that support the inside of a wheel

street-legal approved to be driven on public streets

V-8 engine a large type of engine with eight cylinders arranged in a V pattern

FIND OUT MORE

BOOKS

The Automobile
Edited by Craig Cheetham
(Amber Books, 2007)
With photos of more than 250 cars, this book covers cars from
many nations and all eras.

Eyewitness Cars
Edited by Elizabeth Baquedeno and Richard Sutton
(DK, 2005)
From the earliest models to today's hottest supercars,
this book includes dozens of pictures of cars from around
the world.

365 Cars You Must Drive
By Matt Stone and John Matras
(Motorbooks International, 2006)
An A-to-Z trip around the world of cars, from the Model T to
today's hottest rides. The authors give history tips, discuss
engines, and even include some car songs.

WEB SITES

Visit our Web site for lots of links about classic cars:
www.childsworld.com/links

Note to Parents, Teachers, and Librarians: We routinely check our Web links to
make sure they're safe, active sites—so encourage your readers to check them out!

INDEX

JAMES BUCKLEY, JR. has written more than 60 books for young readers on a wide variety of subjects. He was inspired to write this book by his son Conor, whose love of cars is legendary among his friends and family! Unfortunately for Conor, James just drives a boring old Toyota!